Mom's Favorite Recipes
By Carmen Basalone

Mom's Favorite Recipes

For over 50 years Carmen Basalone has cooked every day meals and special holiday meals for her family. This book contains some of her recipes that are her children's favorites. She hopes that her children and grandchildren will enjoy creating these recipes in their kitchens.

Bon Appetite!

Mom's Favorite Recipes

Carmen Basalone is a French Canadian who was born in St. Hyacinthe, Canada near Montreal and grew up in Troy, Vermont and Warren, Massachusetts. Some of her recipes, such as Buche de Noel and French Crepes, come from her family heritage. In 1960, when she married Dan Basalone, she became an Italian by marriage. In the early years of her marriage she learned Italian cooking from Dan's Grandma Cronin and his aunt, Josephine Fanucchi. Carmen is an avid cook who always looks for interesting recipes which she adapts to her taste and the taste of her family.

The recipes contained in this book are particular favorites that her children enjoyed and requested over and over through the years. As her children became adults with families of their own, they would ask their mother for her recipes. By sharing the recipes in this book, her children will have them at their fingertips to create in their kitchens.

Cooking favorite meals is just one way that Carmen shows her love for her family. Hopefully, her children and their children will carry on this tradition of expressing love for their families through cooking.

Bon Appetite!

Mom's *Buche de Noel*

Ingredients and Directions: Mix, 2 tablespoons granulated sugar; 2 envelopes of unsweetened chocolate; 1 teaspoon of vanilla; 1/4 teaspoon of baking soda; until thick and smooth and set aside. Beat 4 eggs until foamy; gradually add one cup of granulated sugar and beat until very thick and lemon colored; fold in 1/2 cup of all purpose sifted flour with 1/2 teaspoon of baking soda and 1/2 teaspoon of salt; then quickly fold in the chocolate mixture which you had set aside. Spread the batter in a 15"x10"x1" baking pan that has been greased and lined with wax paper and greased again. Bake in a moderate oven at 375 degrees for 15-18 minutes or until a test toothpick comes out clean. (Do not over bake.) Loosen around the edges and invert cake on a towel sprinkled with confectioners' sugar. Remove paper and trim off the crisp edges. Cool for 5 minutes, then roll up in the towel and put on a cake rack. Cool thoroughly.

Whip, 1 cup of heavy cream; fold in 1/4 cup each of chopped walnuts; add 1/2 teaspoon of vanilla. Unroll cake and spread on the cream mixture. Roll the cake, wrap in a towel and chill.

Ingredients and Directions for Chocolate Frosting: Cream 1/4 cup of softened butter; 2 envelopes of unsweetened no-melt chocolate. Gradually blend in 3 cups confectioners' sugar alternately with about 1/3 cup of milk; and add 1 teaspoon of vanilla. Spread top and sides of the rolled cake with the frosting. Sprinkle the top with coconut shavings tinted with green food coloring.

Mom's *Mrs. T's Chicken Salad*

Salad Ingredients: 1 head of lettuce and 1 head of Romaine lettuce chopped (or two bags of butter lettuce); 1/2 package of won ton skins; 4 chicken breasts or 8 chicken tenders; 3 stalks of green onions; 1/4 cup of white sesame seeds.

Salt and fry the chicken in oil or cook in a microwave oven. Cut the won ton skins into quarter inch wide strips and deep fry in oil until crisp. Drain the deep fried chicken and won ton strips on a paper towel until needed to mix in the salad. Shred or cut the chicken into small pieces.

Salad Dressing Ingredients: 4 tablespoons of sugar; 1 teaspoon of salt; 1/2 teaspoon of black pepper; 4 tablespoons of rice vinegar; Place one Tablespoon of Sesame Oil in a measuring cup and add vegetable oil to equal 1/2 cup. Dissolve this mixture in a sauce pan over a low heat (do not boil). Allow the dressing to cool before adding it to the salad.

Combine cooked chicken, sesame seeds and chopped green onions in a large bowl; mix with the chopped lettuce. Toss the salad mixture with the dressing to taste. Add the won ton skins and lightly toss again.

Note: Carmen likes to serve *Mrs. T's Chicken Salad* with Trader Joe's egg rolls.

Mom's *Old Fashioned Crumb Cake*

Ingredients: 2 and 1/4 cups of sifted all purpose flour; 1/2 teaspoon of salt; 1 teaspoon of cinnamon for the topping; 1/2 teaspoon of cinnamon for the batter; 1 cup of brown sugar packed; 3/4 cup granulated sugar; 2/3 cup of vegetable oil; 1/2 cup of chopped walnuts; 1/2 teaspoon of nutmeg; 1/2 teaspoon of baking soda; 1 teaspoon of baking powder; 1 egg; 1 cup of whole milk.

Directions:
Combine sifted flour, salt and 1/2 teaspoon of cinnamon in a large bowl. Add brown and granulated sugars and oil. Mix until fluffy or use an electric mixer. Measure out 3/4 cup of this mixture and set aside for the topping. Add baking soda, baking powder, egg and milk to the remaining flour mixture and mix until smooth.

Combine the topping by adding the chopped nuts, nutmeg and 1 teaspoon of cinnamon to the 3/4 cup of the mixture that was set aside.

Put the batter mixture into a well greased 9"x13" baking pan. Level the top and sprinkle with the topping mixture. Bake at 350 degrees for about 30-35 minutes and check with a toothpick.

Note: *The Old Fashioned Crumb Cake* is best served warm.

Mom's *Hershey Brownies*

Batter Ingredients: 1 cup of granulated sugar; 1 cup of all purpose flour; 1 stick of margarine or salted butter (softened); 4 eggs; 1 can of Hershey's syrup; chopped walnuts are optional to taste.

Directions: Cream the sugar, soft margarine or butter and eggs, one egg at a time. Add syrup, flour and (nuts - optional). Bake in a 9"x13" pan or on a cookie sheet at 350 degrees for 30 minutes.

Frosting Ingredients: 2/3 cup of granulated sugar; 3 tablespoons of margarine; 3 tablespoons of whole milk; 1/4 cup of chocolate chips.

Directions: Place sugar, milk, margarine in a small sauce pan. Bring to a boil and boil for 1 minute. Remove from the heat and add the chocolate chips. Stir to frosting consistency to spread. Apply frosting to brownies while the brownies are still warm. Allow to cool and cut into squares.

Note: Mom enjoys her *Hershey Brownies* with a cold glass of milk.

Mom's *Italian Pizzelles*

Batter Ingredients:
6 eggs beaten; 2 cups of granulated sugar; 1 and 1/2 cups of salted butter or margarine, melted; 1 and 1/2 cups of all purpose flour; 2 teaspoons of baking powder; 4 teaspoons of anise extract; 1 teaspoon of vanilla.

Directions:
Add and beat ingredients together in the order listed. Batter should be thick but flow from a spoon. Place about one tablespoon of batter in the center of your Pizzelle Maker that has been preheated. Close the Pizzelle Maker lid. Allow to cook until steaming stops, about 45 - 60 seconds. Remove with a fork. Allow to cool on a wire rack or towels. Dust with confectioner's sugar after removal from the Pizzelle Maker. Store in airtight containers.

Note: Mom likes thin pizzelles. Pizzelles have been a traditional Italian Christmas holiday treat.

Mom's *French Crepes*

Ingredients: 1 cup of all purpose flour with a "pinch" of salt; 4 eggs beat light; 1 cup of whole milk; 1 cup of water; 2 tablespoons of melted unsalted butter.

Mixing Directions: Place the flour/pinch of salt mixture in a large bowl; Beat the eggs lightly; Add the cup of milk and cup of water to the eggs and beat to mix well; Stir the milk/water/egg mixture into the flour and beat smooth.

Directions: Refrigerate for at least one hour. The batter should be the texture of heavy cream and stir before ladling. Heat a small 5-6 inch skillet or crepe pan (until a drop of water dances on it). Brush the skillet or crepe pan with butter. Ladle in 2 tablespoons of batter. Quickly tilt and rotate pan to spread the batter evenly over the entire bottom of the skillet or crepe pan. Cook about 1 minute or until edges are a light brown. Flip the crepe over and cook the second side. The crepe should be lacy, have some holes, and be soft and rollable. Mom stacks them on top of each other and covers them with a towel to keep warm. This recipe should make about two dozen crepes.

Note: The crepes can be made ahead and refrigerated. The crepes can be used with either a sweet or savory filling. Mom usually spreads maple syrup on the crepes and rolls them up with a fork in lieu of a filling.

Mom's *Scallops in Mushroom Sauce*

Ingredients: 3 tablespoons of margarine or unsalted butter (divided); 2 tablespoons or corn oil or canola oil; 1 pound of scallops (quartered if large scallops); Salt; Freshly ground pepper; 2 tablespoons of finely chopped shallots or onions; 1 large clove of garlic finely chopped; 8 ounces of canned mushrooms; 1/2 cup of dry white wine; 1 can of petite diced tomatoes; 1 tablespoon of fresh parsley, finely chopped.

Directions: In a large skillet, melt 2 tablespoons of butter with the corn or canola oil over medium heat. Add scallops and cook with frequent stirring for about 2-3 minutes (scallops cook quickly, so don't overcook or the scallops will become tough). With a slotted spoon, transfer the scallops to a dish. Sprinkle the scallops with salt and the freshly ground pepper.

Add the remaining tablespoon of butter to the skillet. Stir in the shallots and garlic. Cook for 1 minute. Add the mushrooms and cook by stirring frequently for about five minutes.

Add the wine, tomatoes, and parsley and bring to a simmer. Cook for 4-5 minutes or until some of the liquid has evaporated. Return the scallops to the skillet and stir gently. Cook for 2-3 minutes until heated. Taste for seasoning, add salt and pepper if needed. Mom serves the scallop mixture over linguine or fettuccine pasta.

Mom's *Marinated Flank Steak*

Meat: 2 lbs. of flank steak.

Marinade Ingredients:

1 teaspoon of Adolph's Meat Tenderizer
1 tablespoon of granulated sugar
2 tablespoons of dry sherry wine
2 tablespoons of soy sauce
1 tablespoon of honey

Directions:

Mix the marinade ingredients in a bowl until the sugar and honey are dissolved and incorporated in the marinade.

Prepare the flank steak by trimming excess fat and removing the silver membrane. Pierce the steak at 1 inch intervals Marinate the steak in a plastic bag for at least 4-6 hours in the refrigerator. Broil or BBQ the flank steak about 6 minutes on each side.

Note: Mom usually serves the flank steak sliced across the grain with buttered noodles.

Mom's *Stuffed Flank Steak*

Ingredients:

2 tablespoons of unsalted butter or margarine; 1 medium onion chopped; 3 cups of soft bread crumbs; 1/2 teaspoon of poultry seasoning; 1/2 teaspoon of salt; Dash of pepper; 3 tablespoons of hot water; 1 egg well beaten; 2 pound flank steak; 2 tablespoons of salad oil; 1/2 cup of boiling water.

Directions:

Set oven for slow, about 325 degrees. Melt butter in a 10 inch skillet. Add the onion. Cook until golden brown. Add bread crumbs, poultry seasoning, salt, dash of pepper, 3 tablespoons of hot water and the well beaten egg. Mix well. Spread the mixture on the flank steak that has had excess fat and the silver membrane removed. Roll up the steak like a jelly roll. Tie the rolled up steak securely with string. Brown the meat roll on all sides. Sprinkle with additional salt and pepper. Place the browned roll of meat in a baking dish and add the 1/2 cup of boiling water. Cover and bake for 1-1/2 hours at 325 degrees or until the meat is tender.

Note: This recipe usually makes 6-8 servings. Mom usually served her stuffed flank steak with asparagus or other vegetables.

Mom's *Double Pie Crust*

Ingredients:

2 cups of Sifted Regular Flour
1 teaspoon of Salt
3/4 cup of Crisco
1/4 cup of Water

Directions:

Sift flour before measuring; spoon lightly into measuring cup and level without shaking or packing down. Combine flour and salt in a mixing bowl. With a pastry blender or two knives, cut in the Crisco until uniform; mixture should be fairly coarse. Sprinkle with water a little at a time and toss with a fork. Work dough into a firm ball with your hands. Divide dough into two parts. Roll out one part for the base and sides of the pie pan and the other part for the top of the pie. Bake according to the time and temperature recommended for Mom's Apple Pie Filling.

Note: The double pie crust can be used with other fillings. Check time and temperature for other fillings as needed. This recipe can also be used for two single crust pie shells for open faced pies such as a chocolate pie.

Mom's *Pork Tenderloin with White Wine Sauce*

Ingredients:

10-12 Ounces of pork tenderloin trimmed and cut into 1 inch thick rounds.
2 teaspoons of all purpose flour
1/4 cup (1/2 stick) of unsalted butter
1 large shallot, chopped
1 can of sliced mushrooms, drained
1/8 teaspoon of dried rosemary, crumbled
1/4 cup of dry white wine
1/4 cup of chicken broth
Salt and pepper for seasoning

Directions:

Pat pork tenderloin dry. Place flour in a large plastic bag. Season pork tenderloin rounds with salt and pepper and place in flour bag and shake. Melt butter in a large skillet over medium heat. Add pork and shallots and cook for 4 minutes. Turn pork over to brown both sides. Add mushrooms and rosemary and cook until mushrooms are just soft, about 1 minute. Mix in wine and broth and simmer until pork is cooked through, about 3 minutes. Serve with roasted or mashed potatoes and vegetables.

Mom's *Meatballs*

Ingredients:

1 lb. Ground Beef
3 tablespoons Romano or Parmesan Cheese
2 tablespoons Parsley - Chopped
3 Eggs Slightly Beaten
3 Slices of White Bread
1 Clove of Garlic - Chopped
Salt and Pepper

Directions:

Soak bread in water for about five minutes; then squeeze dry. Mix the soaked bread with all of the ingredients listed above. Shape into balls and roll in flour. Fry in hot oil, preferably olive oil, about 10 minutes or until browned. May be browned under a broiler, but if the broiler is used, do not roll in flour.

Note: Browned meatballs can be put into Mom's Spaghetti Sauce, but the sauce will need to simmer with the meatballs for about an hour.

Mom's *Spaghetti Sauce*

Ingredients:

3 cans of Tomato Paste (6 oz. Cans)
3 tablespoons of Olive Oil
1 Medium Onion - Chopped
3 Cloves of Garlic - Chopped
2 teaspoons of Oregano and 2 Teaspoons of Basil or
2 tablespoons of Italian Seasoning
Salt and Pepper to Taste

Directions:

Saute onions and garlic in olive oil. Add tomato paste and seasoning(s) while stirring to mix. Slowly add 2 cups of water for every can of tomato paste (6 cups of water). Simmer over low heat for at least an hour.

Note: Browned meatballs need to simmer for about an hour in the sauce, but other meat such as browned country ribs will require that the sauce simmer longer in order to fully cook the meat.

Mom's *Italian Sausage (Grandma Cronin's Recipe)*

Ingredients:

5-6 lbs. Pork Butt or Pork Shoulder
Hog Sausage Casings in Salt
Red Chili Pepper Flakes to Taste
Ground Fennel Seeds to Taste
Anise Seeds to Taste; Salt to Taste

Directions:

Cut pork into small pieces (remove excess fat and gristle, but leave enough fatty pieces so that the sausage will have fat for cooking). Add salt, red chili pepper flakes, ground fennel seeds, anise and anise seeds (there are no exact measurements; so start with at least a tablespoon each). Add 1/4 cup of water and mix thoroughly. Let rest in a covered pan for at least 3-4 hours or overnight. Fry a small amount in a little olive oil and taste to see if more seasoning is needed and season to taste. Stuff the meat into the casings and tie off occasionally for desired lengths by using sewing thread. Prick the stuffed casing with a pin multiple times in order to let the moisture escape. Dry sausage links on racks in refrigerator until they turn a dark red color and appear dry and wrinkled. If the sausage is not to be eaten soon, it is recommended to freeze it.

Mom's *Macaroni Salad*

Ingredients:

1 lb. Salad Pasta
5 or 6 Eggs
Mayonnaise
Mustard
3 tablespoons of Sweet Cucumber Slices - Chopped Small
3 tablespoons of Celery - Chopped Small
3 tablespoons of Scallions - Chopped Small
3 tablespoons of Parsley - Chopped Small

Directions:

Boil pasta to tenderness and rinse in cold water. Boil eggs for 10 minutes or until hard boiled and cool in cold water. Put at least a cup of mayonnaise in a small bowl and add a few squirts of mustard, mix until smooth. Place the chopped ingredients into the pasta in a large bowl and toss. Add mayonnaise/mustard and stir. Add mayonnaise if needed to make it rather creamy. Place in a serving bowl and garnish with sliced hard boiled eggs and parsley sprigs. Sprinkle with paprika for color.

Mom's *Potato Salad*

Ingredients:

5-6 Potatoes
5-6 Eggs
1 cup of Mayonnaise
1 teaspoon of Mustard
3 tablespoons of Sweet Cucumber Slices - Chopped Small
3 tablespoons of Celery - Chopped Small
3 tablespoons of Scallions - Chopped Small
3 tablespoons of Parsley - Chopped Small

Directions:

Boil potatoes, cool and then cut up. Boil the eggs at least ten minutes until hard and cool in cold water. Shell the eggs and cut at least ten slices of egg for garnish; the rest of the eggs can be cut up to mix with the potatoes. Mix the mayonnaise and mustard in a small bowl until smooth. Toss the cut up potatoes in a large bowl with the chopped cucumber slices, celery, parsley and scallions. Add the mayonnaise/mustard mixture and stir. Add enough mayonnaise to make it creamy. Place in a serving bowl and garnish with egg slices and parsley sprigs. Sprinkle paprika for color.

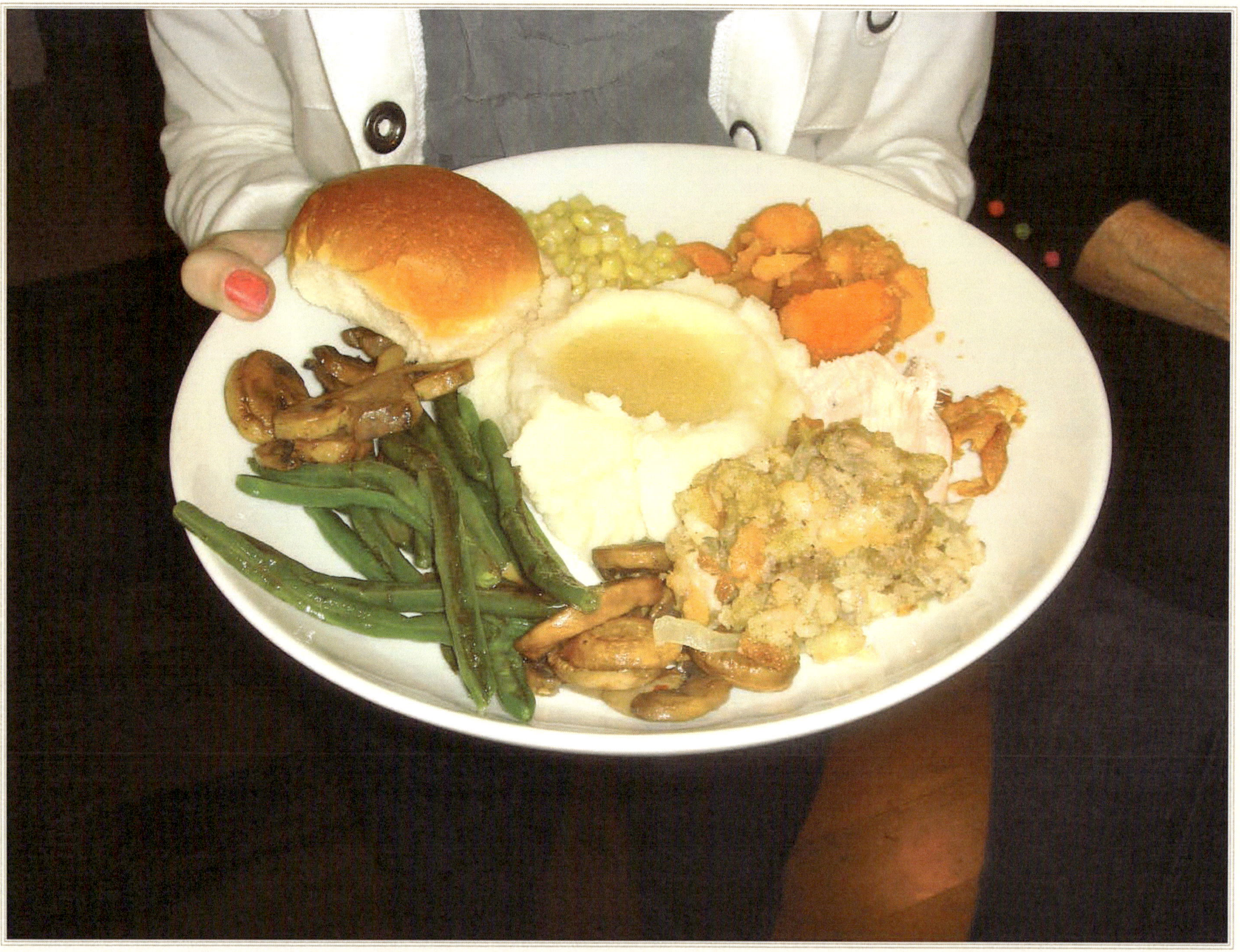

Mom's *Turkey/Poultry Stuffing*

Ingredients:

1 Small Onion
5 tablespoons of Butter
3 cups of Bread Cubes
1 teaspoon of Salt
1/8 teaspoon of Pepper
1 teaspoon of Poultry Seasoning

Directions:

Slice onion and saute in butter until a delicate brown. Add salt, pepper and poultry seasoning to the bread crumbs and then mix well with the sauteed onions. Stuff chicken or turkey and roast for 22-25 minutes per pound at 450 degrees for the first 15 minutes and then at 350 degrees for the remainder of the time.

Note: If you make the stuffing the night before using, be sure to keep it in the refrigerator (Do not stuff it in the turkey). Use a whole fryer or a roaster chicken. This amount is for a roaster chicken, and the recipe will have to be multiplied according to the size of a turkey.

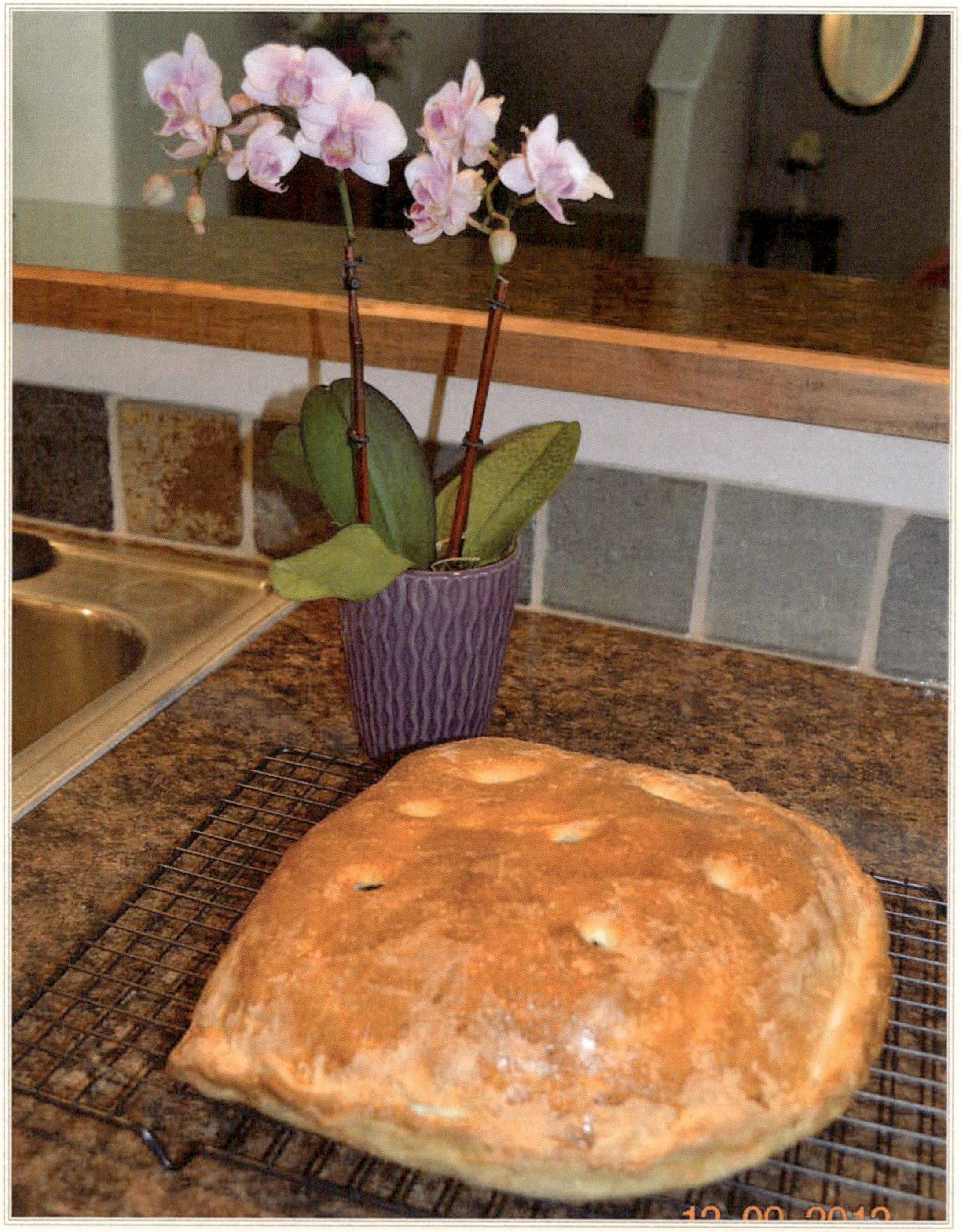

Mom's *Easter Bread*

Ingredients:

1 lb. Ground Italian Pork Sausage - Hot or Mild to Taste
1 lb Ricotta Cheese
1 Egg
1/4 cup of Grated Parmesan Cheese
1 Loaf of Frozen Bread Dough

Directions:

Drain ricotta cheese in cheese cloth overnight. Start by browning the sausage meat and let cool (also drain any fat from the meat). Slightly beat the egg and mix into the ricotta cheese. Add the parmesan cheese to the ricotta cheese. Mix the drained sausage meet into the ricotta cheese.

Place the frozen dough on a baking sheet. Spray all sides of the frozen dough with olive oil. Let thaw and rise to double in size. As it defrosts, spread dough with fingers to make the loaf wider. When dough has stretched to desired size, spread filling on half of the dough. Wet edges with water and fold other side over the filling. Pinch edges to seal. Poke holes on top for steam to escape. Bake at 375 degrees for 45 min. to 1 hour.

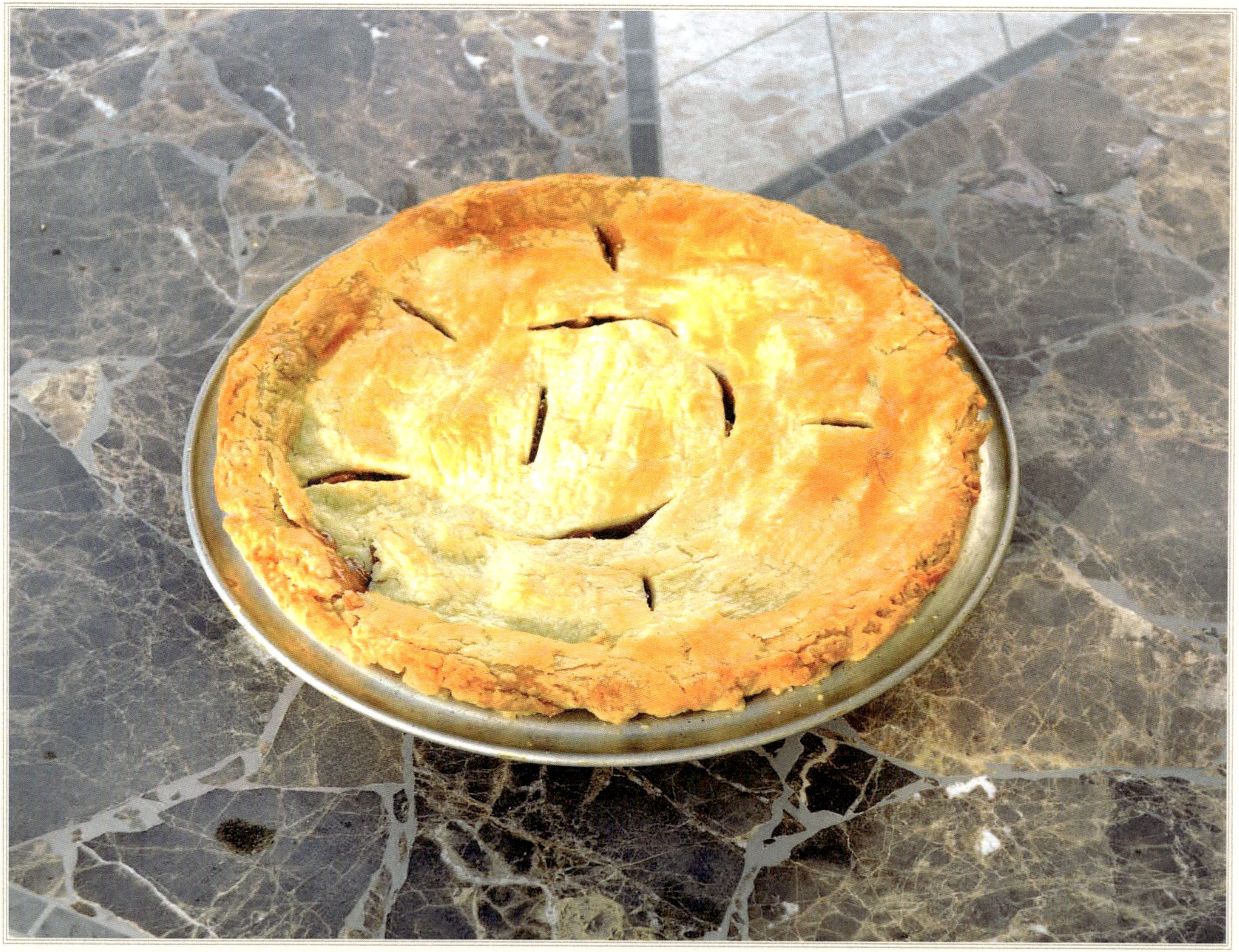

Mom's *Apple Pie*

Filling Ingredients:

6 Medium Apples
2/3 cup of Granulated Sugar; 1/2 Cup of Brown Sugar
1/2 teaspoon of Cinnamon; 1/4 teaspoon of Nutmeg
1/8 teaspoon of Salt; 1 and 1/2 tablespoons of Cornstarch
1 and 1/2 tablespoons of Butter
2 tablespoons of Milk or Cream
1 half of a Lemon; 1 Egg and 1 teaspoon of Water Mixture

Directions:

Prepare double crust using a double crust recipe. Mix the dry ingredients. Peel and slice apples. Mix dry ingredients and milk or cream with the apples. Put apples into the bottom crust. Spread pieces of butter on the apples. Squeeze lemon juice evenly on the apples. Place top crust on the pie. Cut slits in the top crust and finish the edge. Brush top of pie with egg and water mixture. Bake at 450 degrees for 10 minutes; then reduce heat to 350 degrees and bake for 45 minutes.

Note: Crust should be browned and apples should be soft.

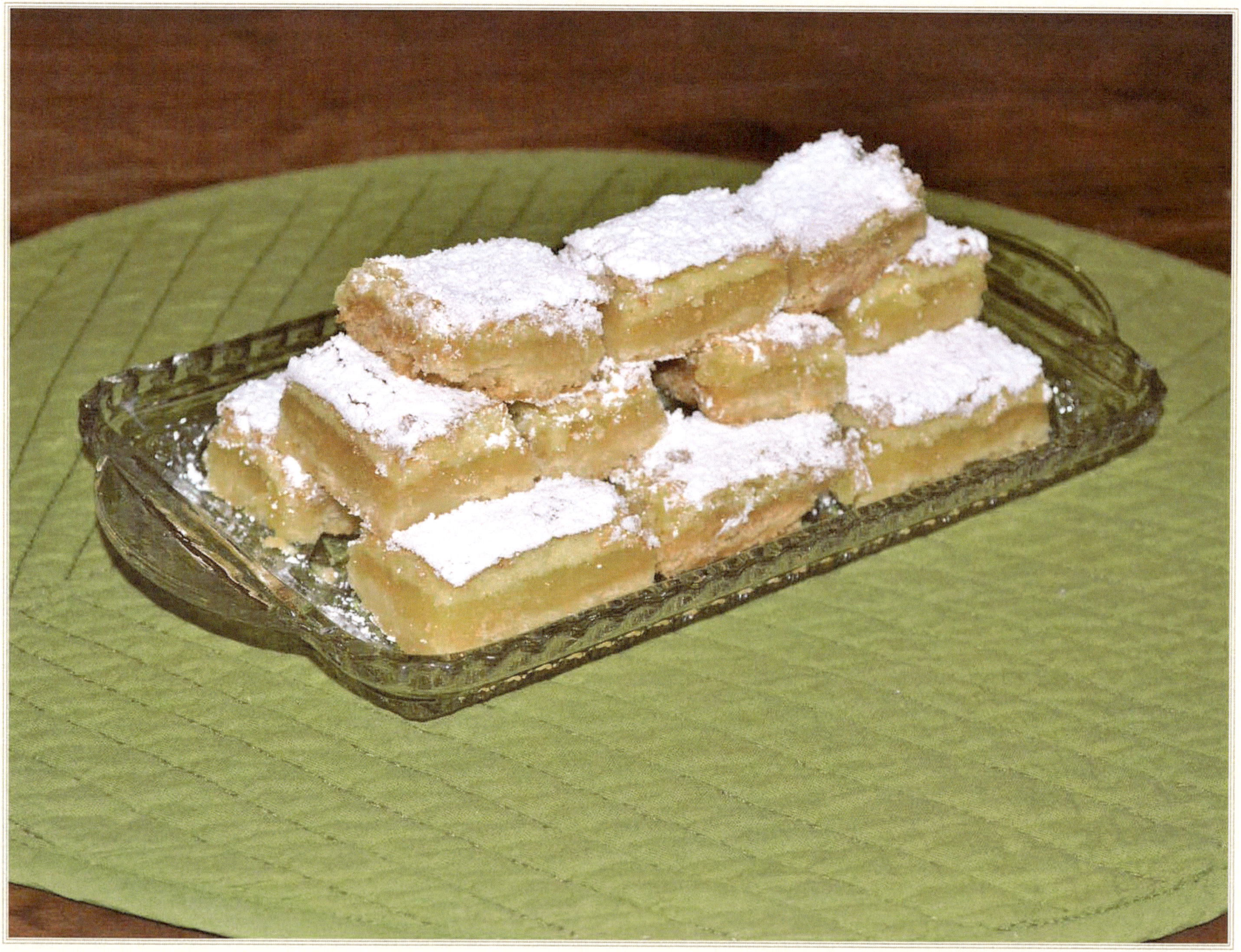

Mom's *Lemon Squares*

Crust Ingredients:

2 cups of Flour
1/2 cup of Powdered Sugar
1 cup of Softened Butter

Directions:

Sift the flour and powdered sugar together. Cut the softened butter into the flour/sugar mixture. Pat evenly in a 13 x 9 inch baking dish at 350 degrees for 25 minutes.

Filling Ingredients:

4 Eggs - Beaten;   2 cups of Sugar - Blended into the Eggs
1/3 cup of Lemon Juice
1/4 cup of Flour;   1/2 teaspoon of Baking Powder

Directions: Beat eggs until foamy, add sugar and lemon juice while continuing beating, add flour and baking powder; mix until smooth and pour over crust; Bake for 25 Min.; Sprinkle with Powdered Sugar

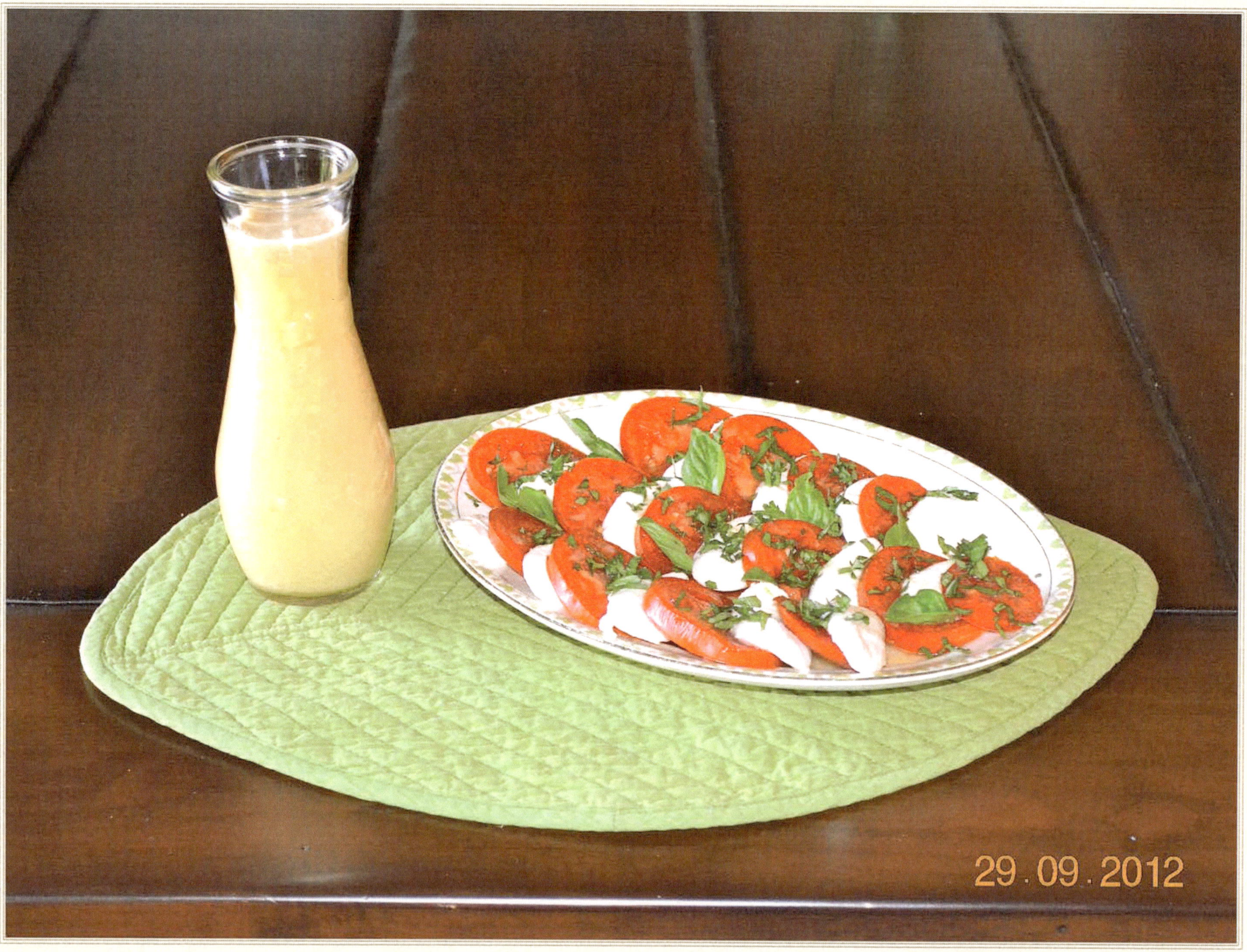
29.09.2012

Mom's *Salad Dressing*

Ingredients:

3 tablespoons of Tarragon Vinegar
2 teaspoons of Lawry's Salt
1 teaspoon of Garlic Powder
3/4 cup of Canola Oil

Directions:

Stir together in a small sauce pan over a low heat to dissolve the seasoning. Stirring occasionally.

Do Not Boil!

Dressing is used for tossed salads and for the tomato and mozzarella with basil salad pictured.

Note: Mom recommends using Heinz Gourmet Tarragon Vinegar.

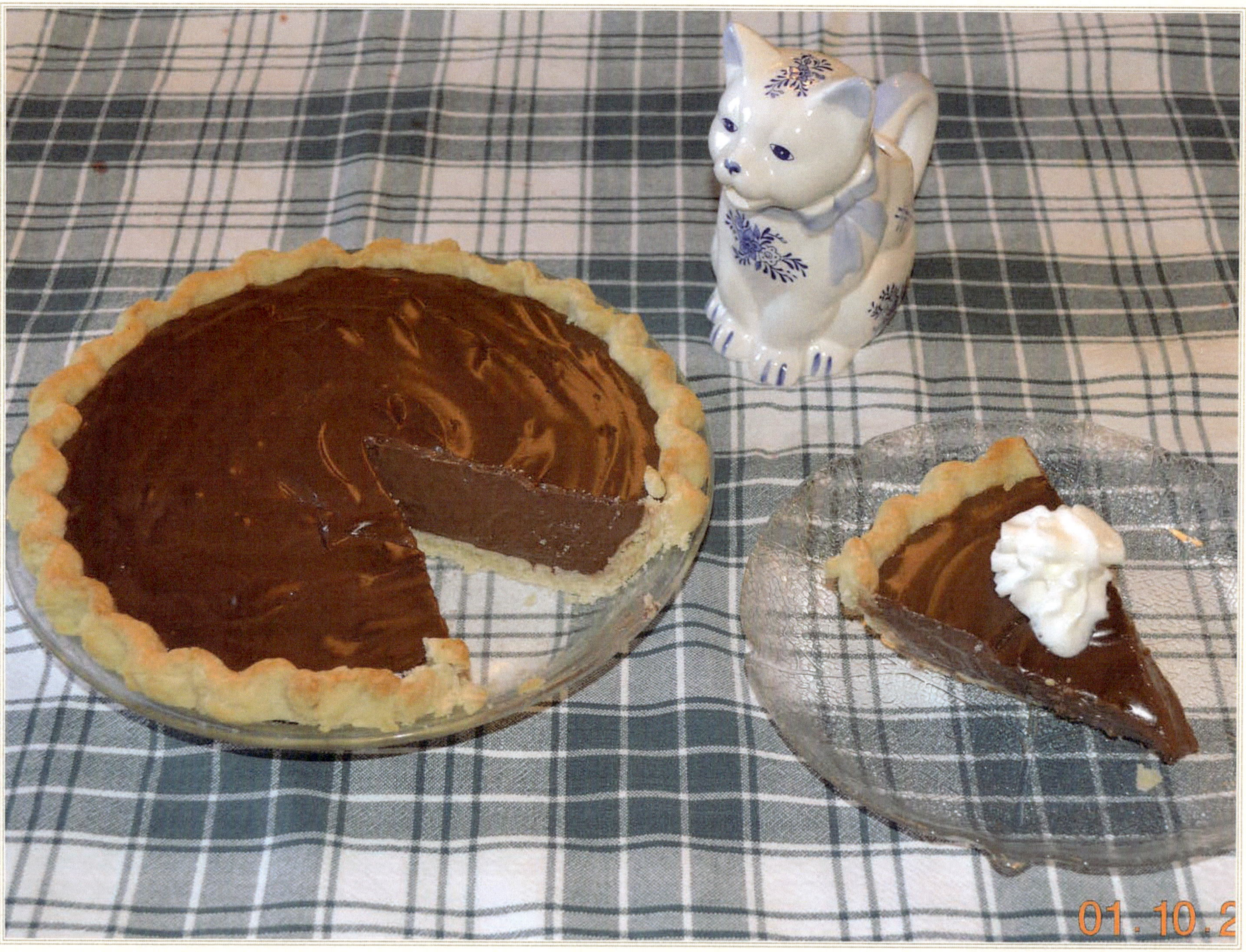
01.10.2

Mom's *Chocolate Pie*

Ingredients:

1 Single Baked Pie Shell
1 Large Box of Cook and Serve Chocolate Pudding Mix
1 Small Box of Cook and Serve Chocolate Pudding Mix
5 cups of Whole Milk

Directions:

Follow the directions for Mom's *Double Crust Pie Shell* recipe. Cook the pudding as directed on the pudding box using whole milk. Place the chocolate cooking pan in cold water to cool the pudding and keep stirring until slightly cooled. By stirring while it cools, this helps to keep the pudding from forming a thick skin. Pour the cooled pudding into the baked pie shell and cool in the refrigerator. Serve with whipped cream topping.

Note: Someone may want to scrape the excess pudding from the pan in which it was cooked. You may have to figure out a system for sharing.

CAFE' LATTE' MOCHA
JAVA MOCHA CAPPUCCINO LATTE
COFFEE LATTE CAPPUCCINO MOCHA JAVA
CAFE' LAT

Mom's *Baked Cabbage*

Ingredients:

1 Head of Cabbage
Extra Virgin Olive Oil
Garlic Salt
Sea Salt or Lite Salt
Pepper
Parchment Paper
Aluminum Foil

Directions:

Cut cabbage into wedges making sure that each wedge has part of the stem in order to keep the wedge from falling apart. Place the wedges on a cookie tray that has been covered with a piece of parchment paper. Brush extra virgin olive oil on both sides of the wedges on the tray. Sprinkle garlic salt on one side of the wedge and sea salt or lite salt and pepper on the other side of the wedge. Cover with aluminum foil and seal around the edges; then, bake in the oven at 425 degrees for 35-45 minutes. Check with a fork to see if tender...give extra time as needed.

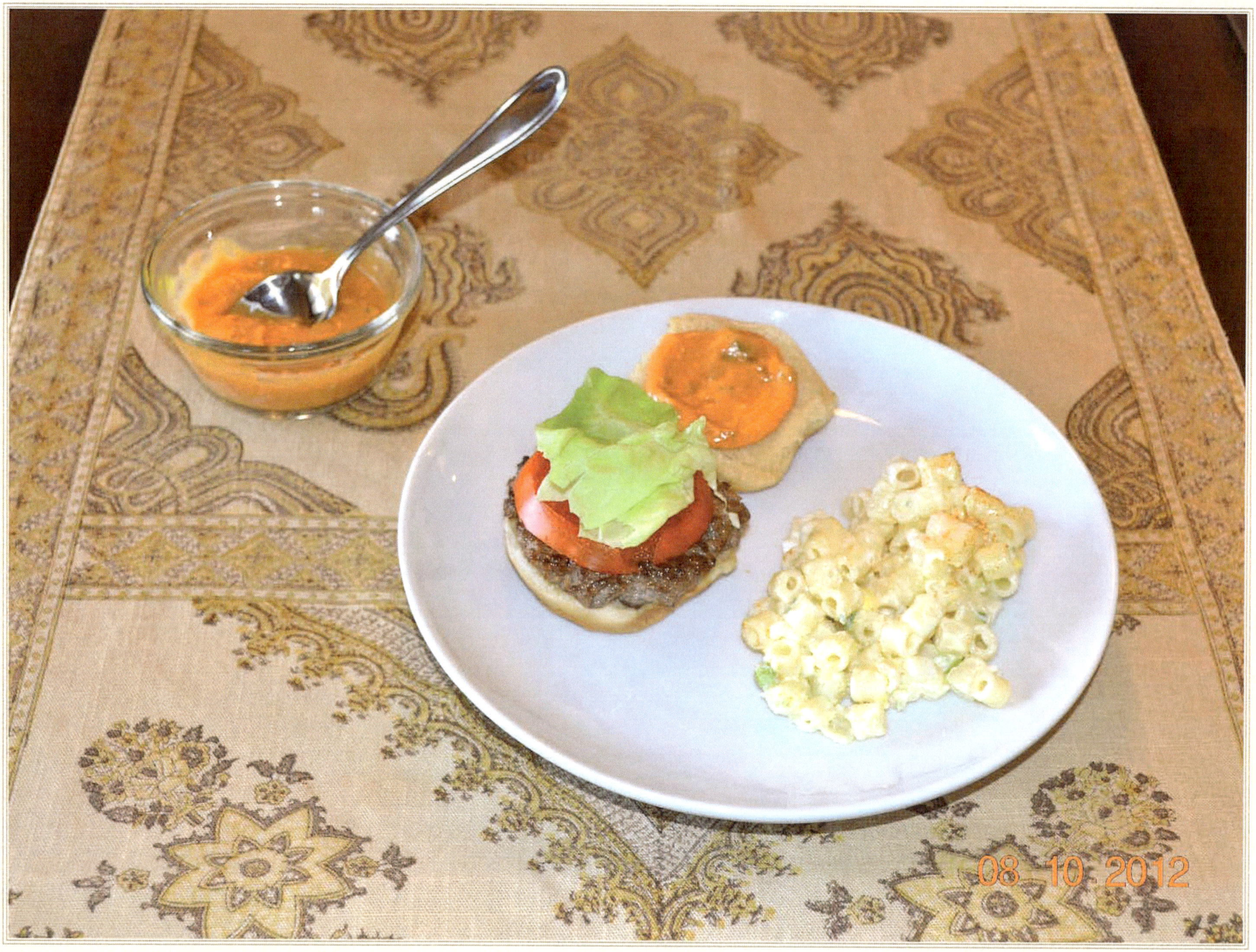
08 10 2012

Mom's *Skyline Grill Secret Hamburger Sauce*

Ingredients:

1 tablespoon of Mayonnaise
2 tablespoons of Catsup
1 teaspoon of Mustard
1 teaspoon of Sweet Pickle Relish

Directions:

Just mix the ingredients together. The amount that you make will depend on the number of hamburgers that you are preparing. For example, you can double or triple the amounts. Have fun experimenting just like Mom did.

Note: The Skyline Grill was the drive-in restaurant that Grandma and Grandpa T. owned in New Port Richey, Florida. The Secret Sauce for hamburgers was Grandma T.'s creation.

50

Mom's *Bean Soup*

Ingredients:

2 cans of White Beans - Drained
1 Ham Bone and Ham Pieces (Mom uses the leftover ham from Easter or other meals)
1 Onion - Chopped
2 Celery Stalks - Chopped
1 Small Can of Tomato Sauce
1 Clove of Garlic - Chopped
4 Strips of Bacon - Cut in Pieces
2 Bay Leaves
Salt and Pepper to Taste
Elbow Macaroni

Directions:

In a pot, cook bacon until crispy; Remove bacon and set aside; Saute onion, celery and garlic. Add ham bone, tomato sauce, bay leaves and cover with water; simmer for 1/2 hour. Add beans, ham pieces, bacon, salt and pepper. Simmer for another 1/2 hour. Meanwhile, boil water to cook elbow macaroni. Drain macaroni and place macaroni in individual serving bowls then ladle the soup over the macaroni.

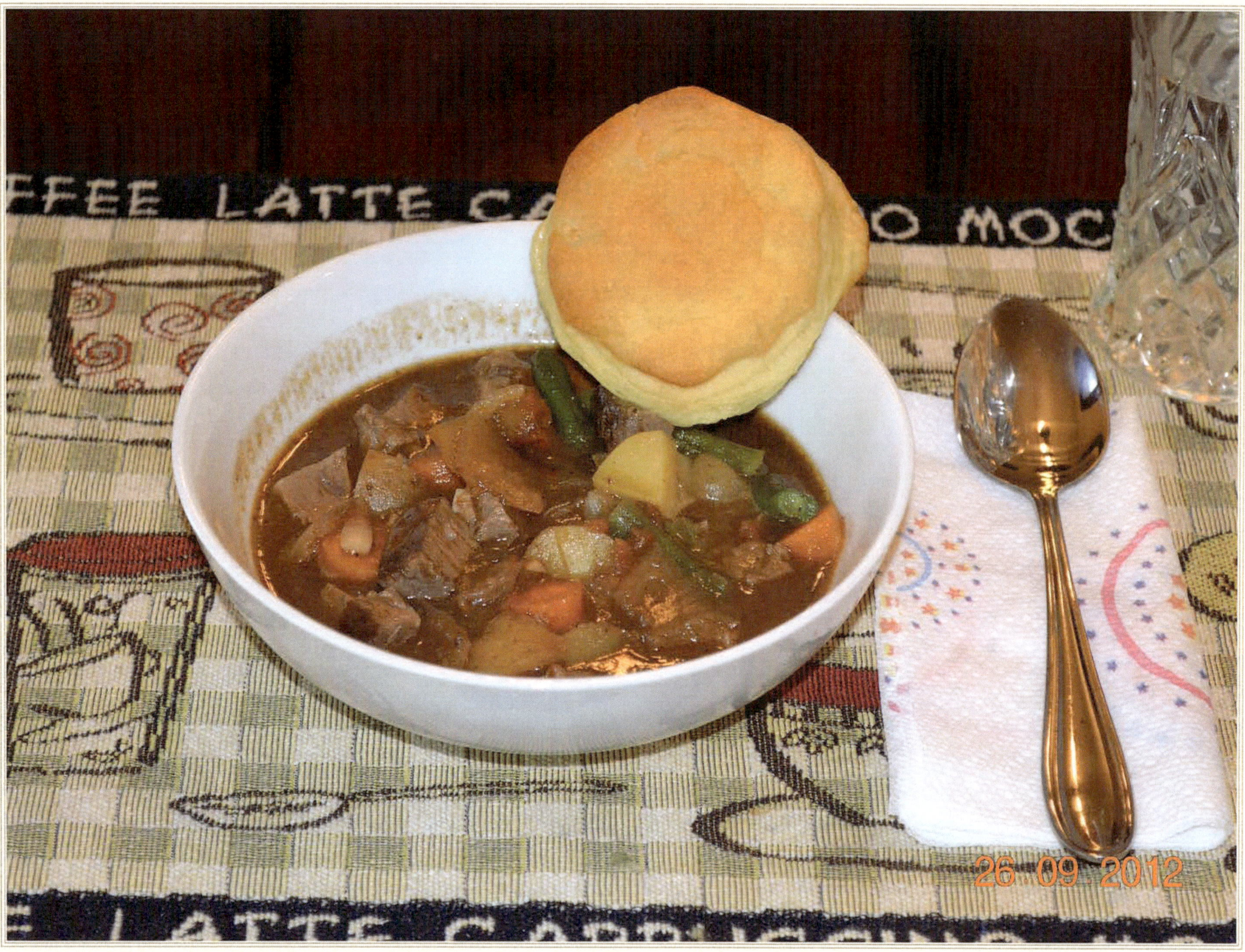
LATTE
26 09 2012

Mom's *Beef Stew*

Ingredients:

1 Pound or more of Top Sirloin or Sirloin Steak - Cubed
Extra Virgin Olive Oil
2 Garlic Cloves - Diced
1 can of Beef Broth
Mushrooms
1 teaspoon of Worcestershire Sauce
1/4 teaspoon of Thyme
1/4 teaspoon of Marjoram
3 Beef Bouillon Cubes
Cut up Carrots, Onions (or Pearl Onions) and Potatoes

Directions:

In a large pot, heat oil and brown meat chunks and garlic. Add beef broth, worcestershire sauce, 3 cans of water, thyme, marjoram and bouillon cubes. Simmer meat for 1 hour; add carrots and simmer for 30 more minutes; add mushrooms, onions and potatoes and simmer for 30 more minutes; Mix 3 Tablespoons of flour with 1/4 cup of water and stir into stew as much as desired for a thicker gravy. Try adding red wine.

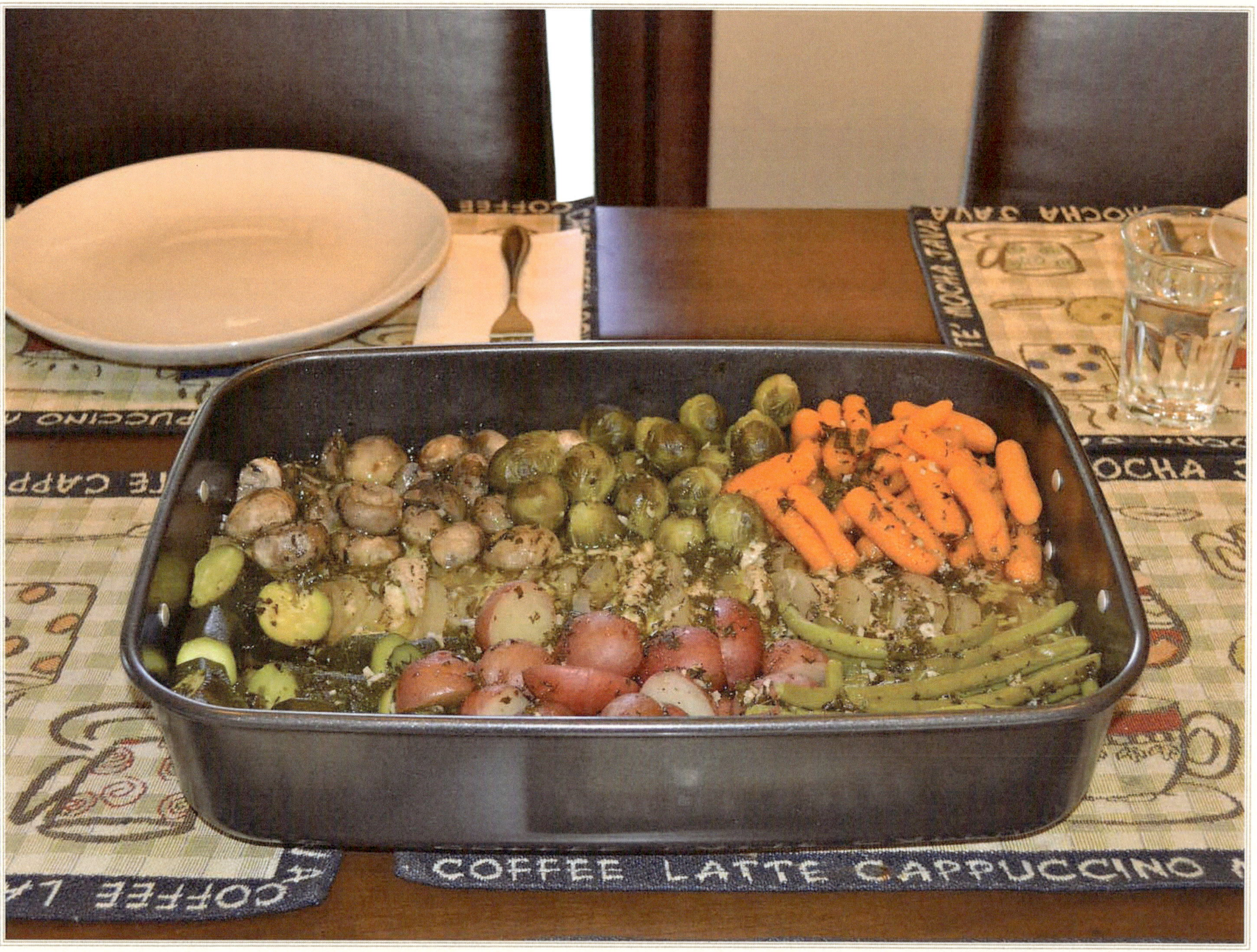
COFFEE LATTE CAPPUCCINO

Mom's *Oven Roasted Chicken and Vegetables*

Ingredients:

Chicken Tenders
1 Small Onion or 1/2 of a Medium Onion - Thinly Sliced
Salt and Pepper to Taste
2 Bay Leaves; 1/2 cup of Parsley - Chopped

Directions:

Salt and pepper chicken tenders and place in center of a roasting pan. Place the sliced onions between the chicken tenders. Arrange any vegetables that you desire, such as new small red potatoes, green beans, carrots, mushrooms, Brussel sprouts or zucchini, around the chicken tenders.

Combine: 1 cup of Dry White Wine; 1/2 cup of Olive Oil; 1 tablespoon of Basil Leaves; 2 teaspoons of Thyme Leaves; 2 teaspoons of Salt; 2 teaspoons of Pepper; 2 Cloves of Garlic - Minced;

Pour the combined ingredients over the chicken tenders and vegetables. Add the Bay Leaves and sprinkle the parsley over the top. Cover and bake at 350 degrees for 1 hour.

23.10.2012

Mom's *Chicken with Penne Pasta*

Ingredients:

3 cups of Broccoli - Cut into Florets
2 cups of Boiling Water; 2 Large Chicken Bouillon Cubes
1/3 cup of Butter; 1/3 cup of Olive Oil; 1/2 teaspoon of Italian Seasoning
2 Cloves of Garlic - Minced; Pinch of Pepper; 1 teaspoon of Salt
2 tablespoons of Bottled Marinara Sauce
1 and 1/2 cups of Flour; 1 and 1/2 lbs. of Chicken Breasts or Tenders - Cut into Strips
1 lb. of Penne or Other Tube Shaped Pasta; Grated Parmesan or Romano Cheese

Directions:

Blanch broccoli florets for 10 seconds and plunge into cold water and set aside. Combine water, bouillon cubes, butter and olive oil in a saucepan then add seasoning, garlic, pepper and marinara sauce; simmer for 10 minutes, stirring occasionally, and set aside. Combine flour and salt in a plastic bag and coat chicken pieces; heat 1/3 cup of olive oil in a skillet over medium heat; add chicken pieces and cook until brown then drain on paper towels to cool. Cook pasta in boiling, salted water and drain. Pour sauce over pasta and mix well. Add broccoli and chicken and mix again. Season with salt and pepper to taste. Serve with grated parmesan or Romano cheese and any remaining sauce.

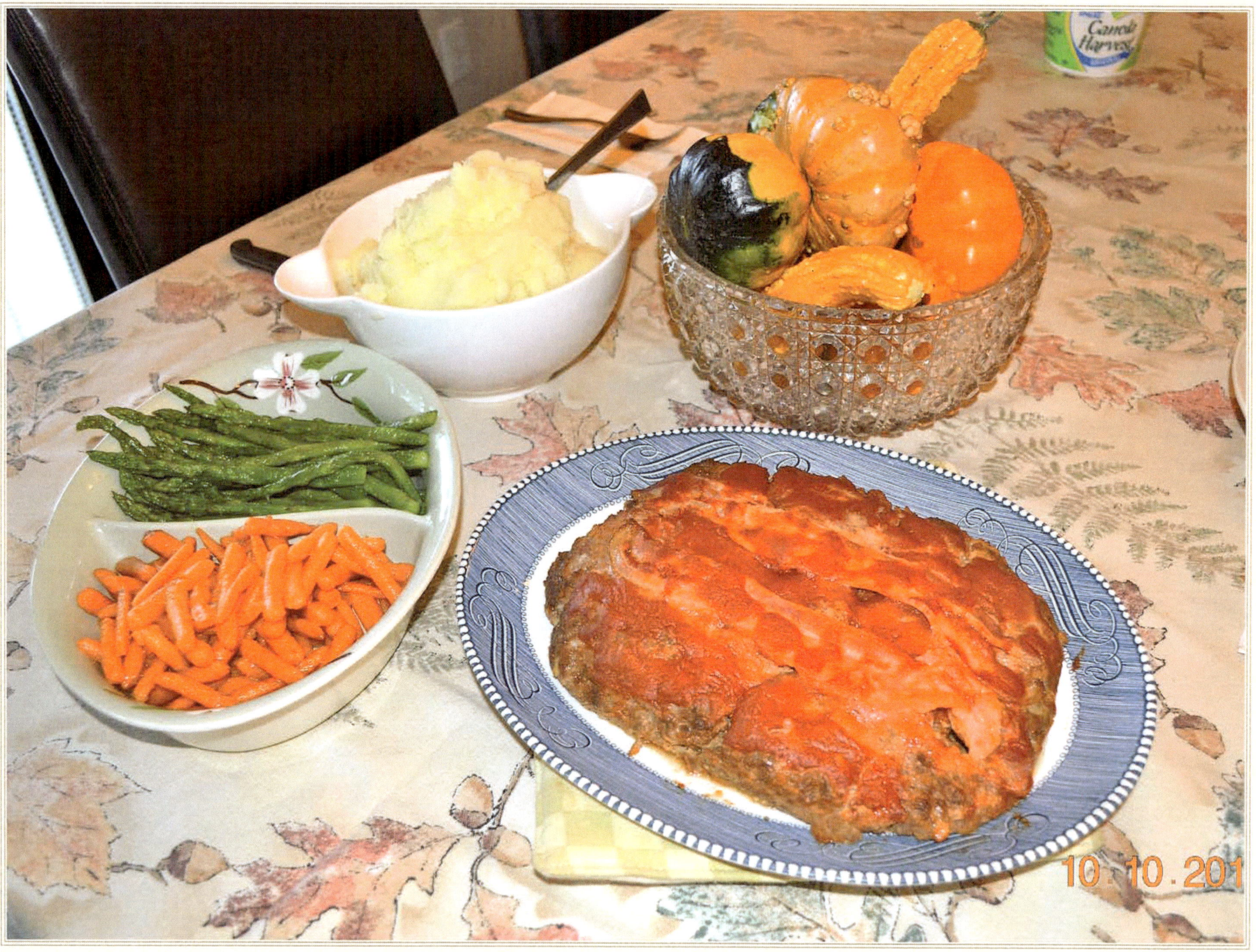
Canola Harvest
10.10.201

Mom's *Meatloaf*

Ingredients:

2 Pounds of Ground Beef
2 Eggs
1 and 1/2 cups of Bread Crumbs
3/4 cups of Catsup
1/2 cup of Water - Warm
1 teaspoon of Accent
1 package of Dry Onion Soup Mix
2 Strips of Bacon
1/2 of 8 ounce can of Tomato Sauce

Directions:

Mix the ground beef, eggs, bread crumbs, catsup, warm water, Accent and dry onion soup mix; then, form into a loaf. Put two strips of bacon on top and pour the tomato sauce over the loaf. Bake for 1 hour at 350 degrees.

Note: Mom usually serves meatloaf with mashed potatoes and corn.

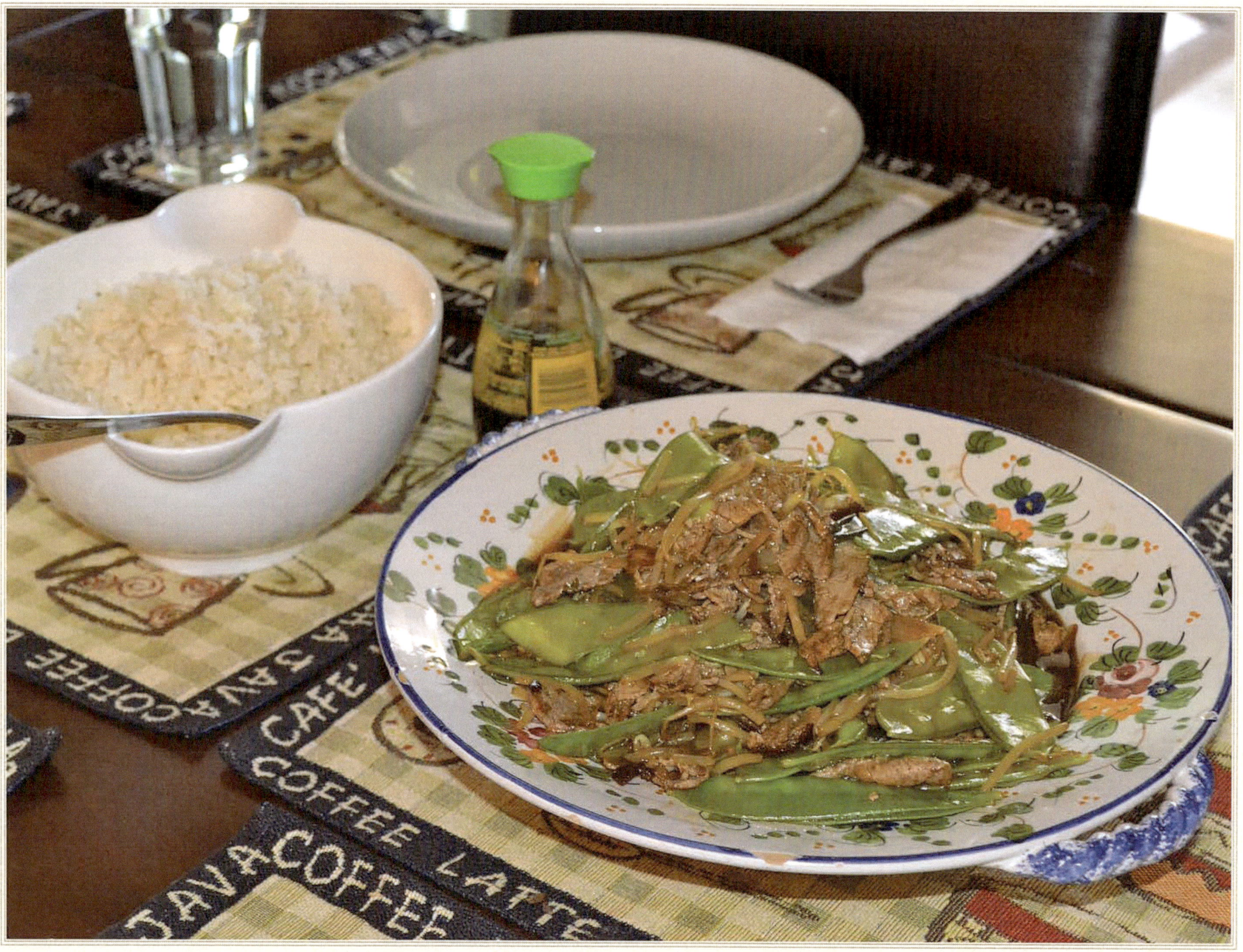
CAFÉ
COFFEE LATTE
JAVACOFFEE

Mom's *Beef and Pea Pods*

Ingredients:

1 Flank Steak
1 teaspoon of Olive Oil
1/2 lb. of Bean Sprouts
1/2 lb. of Snow Peas
1 Bunch of Scallions - Chopped
1 can of Consomme
3 tablespoons of Soy Sauce; 1 teaspoon of Slivered Ginger Root
1 and 1/2 tablespoons of Corn Starch; 2 tablespoons of Cold Water
Salt to Taste; Hot Steamed Rice

Directions:

Slice steak diagonally across the grain and brown in hot oil; then, remove from skillet. Cook rinsed bean sprouts, snow peas and scallions in same skillet for a few minutes. Add undiluted consomme combined with soy sauce and ginger. Cover and cook for two minutes. Stir in corn starch mixed with cold water. Cook and stir until clear and thickened. Add meat strips and mix lightly to coat well with the sauce. Add salt to taste. Serve over the hot steamed rice. Makes about six servings.

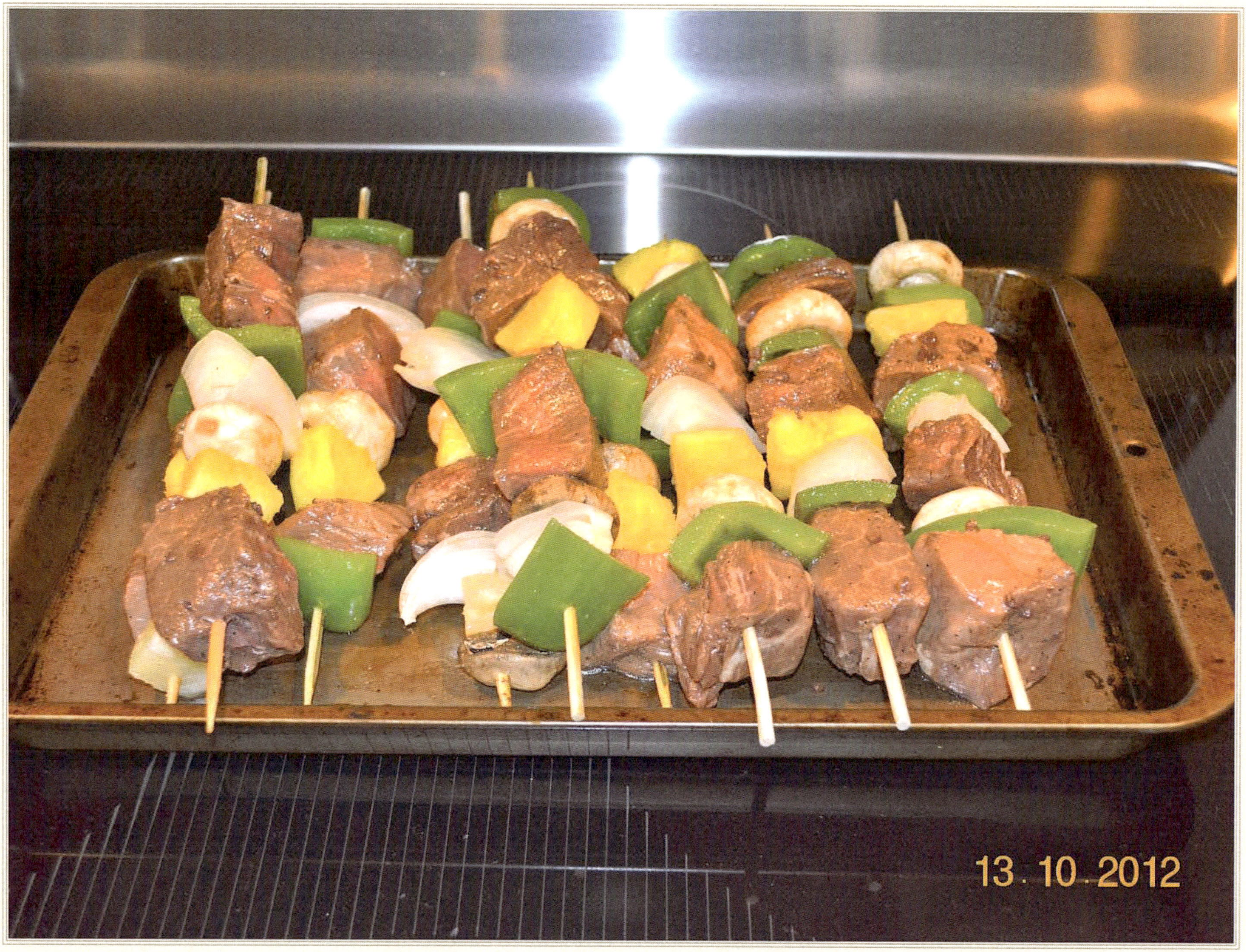
13.10.2012

Mom's *Shish Kabob Marinade*

Ingredients:

1/4 cup of Canola or Vegetable Oil
1/2 cup of Red Wine
1 Garlic Clove - Chopped
1 teaspoon Onion - Chopped
1/2 teaspoon Salt
1/2 teaspoon Pepper
1 tablespoon Worcestershire Sauce

Directions:

Cut top sirloin or sirloin steak into 1 and 1/2 to 2 inch cubes and place in a large ziplock baggie. Mix the ingredients for the marinade and pour over the steak pieces in the ziplock baggie. Place in the refrigerator to marinate for at least one hour. Skewer the steak cubes with pieces of bell pepper, onions, mushrooms and pineapple and grill according to taste.

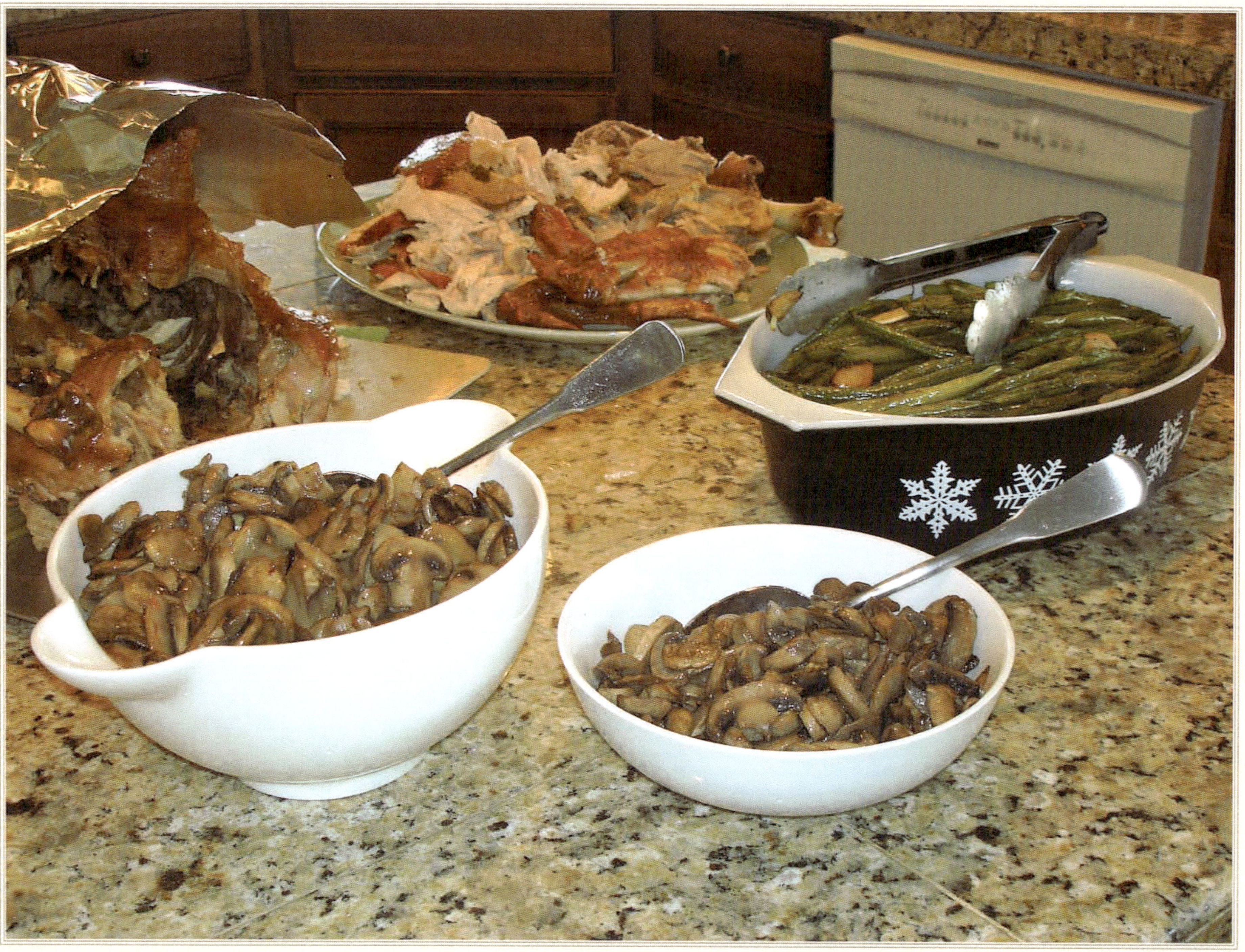

Mom's *Sauteed Green Beans and Mushrooms*

Ingredients:

Fresh Green Beans
Fresh Mushrooms
Extra Virgin Olive Oil
Sliced Garlic
Salt and Pepper
Chili Flakes or Butter

Sauteed Green Bean Directions:

Blanch green beans until soft but still crunchy; Heat olive oil and fry one or two slices of garlic; Remove garlic when browned; add enough green beans to cover the bottom of the skillet, saute until slightly browned; Place green beans on paper towel to remove excess oil; add salt, pepper and the roasted garlic; Repeat with rest of green beans and garlic.

Sauteed Mushrooms:

Heat olive oil and fry one or two cloves of garlic until brown, then add sliced, dry mushrooms; Salt while cooking and add chili flakes or butter depending on taste.

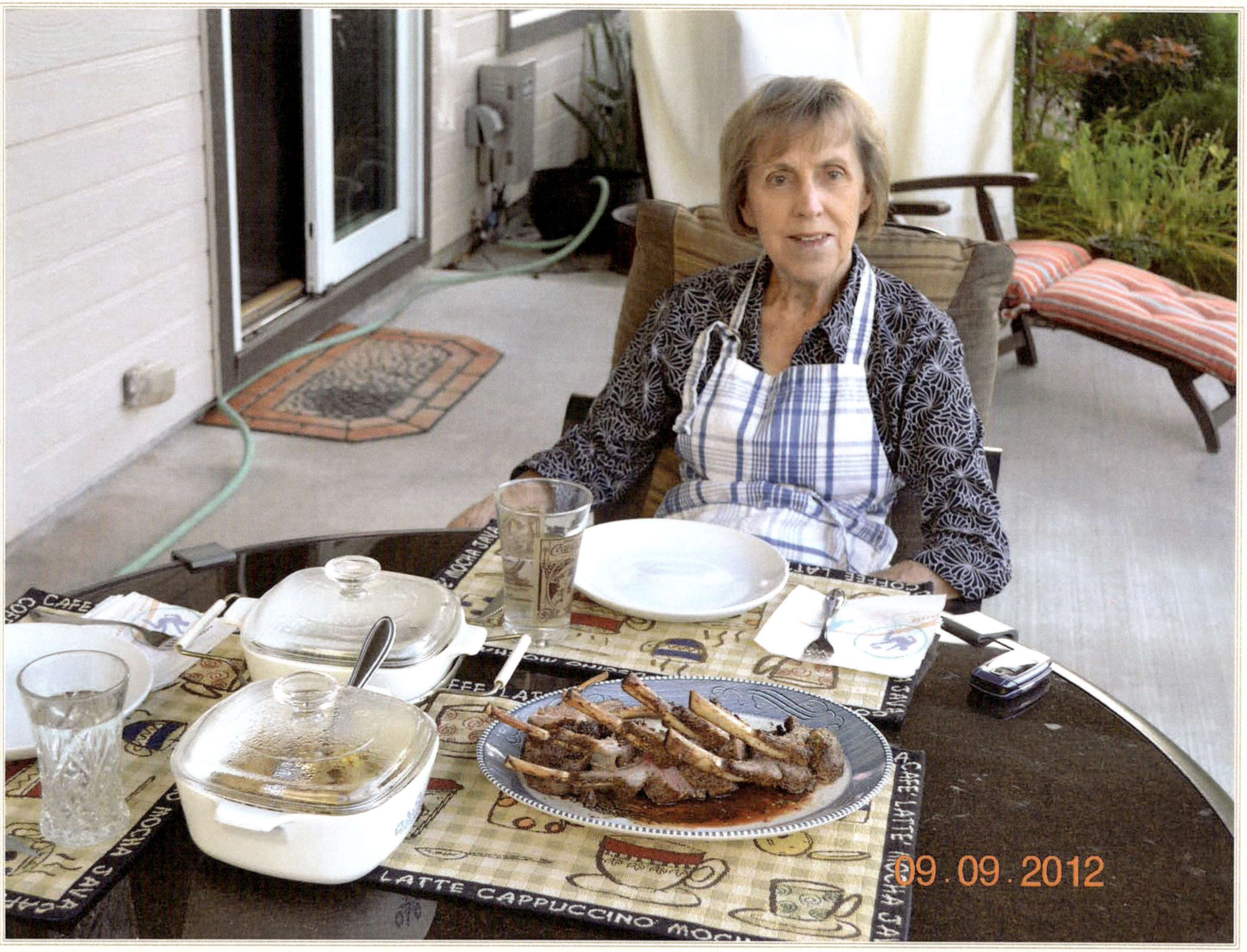
LATTE CAPPUCCINO MOCHA
09.09.2012

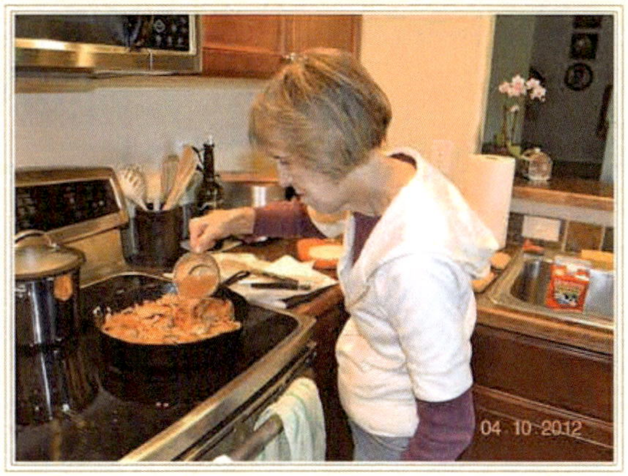
04 10 2012

Mom's Favorite Recipes

Bon Appetite!

Milton Keynes UK
Ingram Content Group UK Ltd.
UKRC032314110824
446710UK00001B/2